ID0686476

The How-to-Hire Handbook for Small Business Owners

ANDREA M. HILL

Mardrea Press

Copyright © 2014 by Andrea M. Hill

All rights reserved. No part of this book may be reproduced or transmitted in any form or by any means, electronic or mechanical, including photocopying, recording, or by any information storage and retrieval system, without permission in writing from the Publisher.

Mardrea Press
Campbellsport, Wisconsin, USA
marketing@mardreapress.com
www.mardreapress.com

Cover Design by SupportWerx
© Mardrea Press
All rights reserved

First Edition, February, 2014

Copyright © Andrea M. Hill, 2014
The How-To-Hire Handbook for Small Business Owners, 111 Pages.
Wisconsin: Mardrea Press, 2014
1st ed.

Library of Congress Control Number: 2014901937

ISBN - 10: 0615959350
ISBN - 13: 978-0-615-95935-1

Acknowledgement

This book would not be possible without my life partner Marlaine. She has helped develop and refine these hiring concepts over the years, she is my first and best proof-reader, the kindest yet most thorough of critics, and she keeps our lives together in every way. To say this book would not have been possible without her is an understatement.

About the Author

Andrea Hill has a long history of successful business development and management, from being a senior member of a major publishing house management team, to CEO of an international clothing design firm, to CEO of one of the world's largest jewelry distributors and manufacturers. In 2007 she formed Hill Management Group with the intention of distilling her corporate experience into tools and knowledge that would provide small business owners with immediate benefit. If you want all the details on Andrea's background, you can find her online resume at www.linkedin.com/in/andreahillconsulting.

Andrea has expert knowledge in strategic development, branding, marketing, leadership development, human resources, operations design, lean manufacturing, quality systems, and strategic measurement. She is regularly published in the business press, has written and delivered dozens of management development programs, and excels at leading executive teams through strategic development processes.

But the most important thing to know about Andrea is that she believes small business is the backbone of North American commerce. "Small business accounts for the vast majority of our employment, opportunity creation, and innovation," she says. "I can think of no nobler thing to do with the latter half of my career than bring everything I have learned to the service of these brave people who wake up every day and create opportunity for themselves and others. Is that overly dramatic? I don't think so. Small business is the embodiment of our shared pioneer spirit. It's important, it's exciting, and it's what I do best."

Table of Contents

Prelude: We Begin

One of the most challenging aspects of any business is the hiring, training, and fostering of employees. Hiring a new employee is nerve-wracking. Even the most exemplary candidates cost in terms of additional wage expense, training time, attention, and inevitable mistakes. Perhaps of even greater concern to most small business owners, adding a new person changes the culture. So it's no wonder that most people put off hiring until the last possible moment.

But what happens when you can't put it off any longer? What happens when the company is suffering more from the lack of help than from the potential risks of bringing in new help? At that point you must attract, interview, hire, train, and incorporate a new person into your organization. How you do those things will make the difference between a good outcome and a terrible one.

This handbook will walk you through the most important things you must consider, understand, and do when it's time to hire. So let's get to it! There's a good chance you've waited too long already.

Deciding What Help You Need
. . . and When You Need It

If you're like most small business owners, you realize you must hire someone (or at least, you finally *accept* you must hire someone) when you haven't slept for three days straight. I don't judge. It happens. And if that's the place you're at right now, you have decided to read the right book.

Ideally, the time to decide when to hire and what type of help to hire is before the need to hire has throttled your productivity. How do you do that? With two types of planning: Strategic Planning and Skills Planning.

Business Strategy Comes First

The first type of planning you must have in place is your business strategy. To plan your hiring needs in advance, you must know what you are trying to accomplish with your business and in what time frame. For instance, if you have a business plan to grow 15% in the next year, which aspects of your business will experience the stress of that growth? Each time you review or update your business plan, you should spend some time considering the implications of your plan for staffing. Here are some questions you should ask today about what your business will be like two years from now:

- Which departments[1] will experience the most growth/strain?

- Which functions[2] will need significant training to meet future needs, and what type of training?

- What types of new talent will you need?

- Are there any aspects of your business plan that can't be accomplished without hiring new people, or which would be accomplished more quickly or more effectively by hiring new people?

- Are there any areas you are currently outsourcing that will make more sense to staff internally?

- How much of your additional revenue and cash flow will need to be dedicated to additional staff?

By asking and answering these questions you will gain insight into the types and numbers of people you will need before the need becomes a reality. As you monitor your actual performance compared to your business plan forecasts, you can speed up or slow down the hiring needs you have identified. The key is to put hiring into your plans and not just approach the need to hire as a reaction.

---

[1] A Department is a section or unit of a business, typically consisting of a manager and/or supervisor and reporting staff, responsible for a specific set of related tasks, such as Advertising, Sales, Production, or Accounting.

[2] A Function is a specific process or operation that is performed routinely in a business. There are typically multiple functions within a department.

Is your current business plan sufficiently developed to inform and guide your future hiring needs? If not, put this on your personal to-do list. A business plan serves many vital purposes, and forecasting hiring needs is at the top of the list.

Skills Planning Comes Next

After business strategy, the key to hiring the right people on time is to know which skills and competencies your company needs. Most businesses understand the importance of forecasting cash flow, projecting inventory requirements, planning for capital, and anticipating the need for more space. But few do an adequate job of forecasting the need for a particular type of job or skill. Here are two simple methods for developing a skills forecast.

The SWOT Method

A SWOT (strengths, weaknesses, opportunities, threats) Analysis is a common tool used for strategic or marketing planning. The typical approach is to brainstorm all the strengths, weaknesses, opportunities, and threats a company has or faces, then develop strategies for bolstering advantages and mitigating problems. But I'm going to show you how to use the SWOT in a much more focused manner to help you plan future skills requirements.

First, make a list of the functional areas of your company. Your list may include Production, Sales, Customer Service,

Accounting, Inventory Management, and Marketing. Using a notebook or loose-leaf paper, give each functional area its own page. Divide each page into four vertical columns, and write **strengths, weaknesses, opportunities**, and **threats** as the headers for the four columns.

- A *strength* is any characteristic of a functional area that gives your business an advantage. This could be a particular talent that your business has and that your competitors wish they had, or perhaps you have specific skills required to use complex technology.

- A *weakness* is any characteristic of a functional area that places that department at a disadvantage. A weakness is usually the absence of an important skill. It can also be having the wrong person in a critical role. Weaknesses have a direct negative effect on productivity.

- An *opportunity* is any element of a functional area – from talent to technology – that you can exploit to your advantage, particularly one that you do not believe your competitors possess.

- A *threat* is any element or issue in the functional area that could cause serious trouble for your business. For example, if you offer a service or a product that is dependent on a particular skill or technology, and you have only one person capable of doing that work, then a significant threat would be the loss of that one person.

	Strengths	Weaknesses	Opportunities	Threats
Customer Service	1st Class CRM	Not enough staff - long wait times	Use CRM to provide even better service	Cant keep up. Customers might ditch us
	Excellent training program	Very long training curve	Shorten the training curve	
	Strong product knowledge	Not using CRM as much as we could		
	Our staff includes known experts			
	Pay aligned with performance			

The key to making a Skills SWOT work is to be very specific; to focus on one function or department at a time. If you try to do the SWOT across all your skills and abilities for the entire company in one pass, your thinking will be too generic. Even if you have only three people in the company, it is important to assess each department or function on its own.

Let's use a *customer service* department as an example. Under the first column heading, list all the strengths your company has in terms of skills and talent to *provide customer service*. Under the second column, list your company's weaknesses in skills and talent for customer service. Repeat for opportunities and threats. Then repeat the entire activity for each of the other department or functional areas. Once you have done this exercise for each department or function, you will have a thorough – and *actionable* – picture of how you must manage your skills development and acquisition in the future.

Completing this exercise will provide insight regarding which areas of the company are sufficiently staffed, which areas must be supplemented with training or hiring, and what opportunities you might be able to pursue if you had better skills in each area. The threats column will indicate if you have any areas which would be particularly damaged if a key person left, if you have exposed yourself to a competitive move by another company with better talent, or if you are already in danger of failing to meet customer expectations due to lack of personnel or insufficient skillsets.

This exercise is also helpful if you have decided to launch a new product or service, or if you are launching any new strategic activities. Planning ahead for skills and talent is essential to success. Too many commercially viable ideas have been tanked due to the lack of sufficient talent to launch them.

The SKILLS Matrix

A Skills Matrix is also a visual tool. Whereas the Skills SWOT helps you identify how you must invest in human resources at the department level, the Skills Matrix helps you identify what you need to do at the individual level.

Also, just like the Skills SWOT, we do the Skills Matrix by department. If you try to do the Skills Matrix across the entire company at once, it becomes unfocused and meaningless, so be sure to do the Skills Matrix one group at a time.

The Skills Matrix is useful for helping you decide how to solve your staffing problems: with training, moving people around, or hiring. Sometimes we think we need to hire, when in fact we have capacity but we are not prepared to use it. The Skills Matrix can identify where improving skills at the individual level can resolve productivity or production problems. It can also provide important insight regarding holes in your staffing that could be filled by hiring, and problems that could be eliminated through replacing an employee with a person with stronger skills or greater interest.

Start by listing the talents, skills, and competencies the department requires down a vertical axis. Across the horizontal axis make a list of employees in that department (even if you only have one employee in a department, do the exercise this way). This tool helps you visualize which areas have sufficient coverage and which do not. By gaining visibility to these skills gaps you can anticipate and prepare for your hiring and training needs much earlier.

Place a rating of 1-5 in the box to indicate current level of skill.

	Mary	Todd	Jackie
Warmth w/ Customers	5	2	3
Entering Orders	4	2	1
Order Research	3	3	2
Product Knowledge	5	5	5
Closing Sales	1	2	2

Rate each employee on their skills using a scale of 1 – 5 (1 being "no skill yet" and 5 being "highly proficient"). This can be a difficult task. You may discover you aren't sure of someone's skill level, or you may not want to be too tough or critical.

Whenever possible, I recommend that you do this exercise with the members of the group or department being rated. If your organization is suffering from any trust or morale problems, then doing the exercise with the group may feel too intimidating to be effective. But if your organization enjoys a sense of openness, and if you are willing to be brutally honest about yourself in the process, you will find that most people are capable of rating themselves fairly and accurately.

The other benefit of doing this exercise with the group is that it introduces a friendly and open form of competitiveness. As your team members participate in this objective exercise, most of them will be motivated to pursue and master more skills.

Once the Skills Matrix is complete, you will gain immediate insight into your staffing strengths, weaknesses, and future needs. You will be able to see the skills or talents that are under-staffed right now, areas that have no coverage at all, and areas in which your coverage is heavier than it needs to be. Once you can see the gaps, you can decide whether you should fill the gaps with training (the earlier you start the better) or if you should hire.

What Skills Should You List on the Matrix?

Of course, *before* you complete your skills matrix you must understand the skills required for each role. Most companies engage in little or no skills assessment. If they do any skills assessment at all, they typically just consider the tasks and activities of the employees. Tasks and activities are important, but did you know that most of the mistakes employees make are due to a lack of broader knowledge, and not due to lack of basic skills?

Here's a terrific example I encounter all the time. Many small businesses retain a CPA or Accountant to review the books at the end of the year, and they entrust the basic bookkeeping tasks to a capable employee – often an employee with administrative skills but lacking traditional bookkeeping skills. The employee is very detail-oriented, trustworthy, and timely in making her bookkeeping entries. But at the end of the year, the Accountant informs the small business owner that her books are "a mess." What has typically happened is that the employee lacks important knowledge about *why* certain types of income or expense need to be categorized in certain ways, or the thought process required to set up a new account. In this example, the basic tasks and activities of the job were being done as expected, but someone with deeper knowledge could see real flaws in the work.

Therefore, when you create your skills lists, you must consider not only which skills are necessary to sustain the company in each functional area, but also the knowledge required to support those skills. The skills should be grouped in the following categories:

- Company Knowledge
- Theoretical Knowledge
- Practical Knowledge
- Skills and Activities.

1. Company Knowledge means knowing about the

company's customers, industry, and competitors in the market. Employees need to understand the company philosophy and brand. They must also understand how their department fulfills its role in expressing the brand, and the relationships between their department and the other departments or functions in the company. These things may be self-evident to you, but don't assume that your employees understand them.

2. Theoretical Knowledge is the business or technical knowledge behind a particular task or skill. For instance, a customer service representative may feel he is serving his company best if he takes a hardline about product returns, not knowing that service flexibility is what leads to loyalty and repeat purchases. Many small businesses have sought employees to manage their social media, only to find out that there's a big difference between knowing how to operate on Facebook and knowing what it means to be an effective marketer. Employees need to understand more than *what* to do. They must also understand *why* you want them to do it, and *how* their tasks and activities affect the company's profitability.

3. Practical Knowledge is the experience one must have or develop in a particular area. How to sell, work with difficult customers, fabricate in gold, run a lathe, manage inventory, run a marketing promotion, coordinate events, provide computer support, and coordinate production are all examples of Practical

Knowledge. This is the type of knowledge that is typically gained through experience. It is made up of things you do, less cerebral than Theoretical Knowledge but broader than Skills and Activities.

4. Skills and Activities are the granular tasks that an employee does in the exercise of their Practical Knowledge. For instance, if the Practical Knowledge is *Sales*, the Skills and Activities may include computer tasks such as *looking up a customer, entering an order, processing a return*, or *issuing a gift certificate*.

A skills list for a customer service department might look like this:

Customer Service Department Skills List

Company Knowledge
- Service philosophy of the company
- Categories of customers and their relative importance
- Your primary competitors
- The relationship of the customer service role to other roles in the company.

Theoretical Knowledge
- The difference between prospects and customers and how to approach them
- Why role differences exist; for example, why customer service has a fostering role and leaves the policing role to accounting
- How prospects, first-time customers, and loyal customers contribute differently to the bottom line of the company.

Practical knowledge
- Technical knowledge regarding your products and services
- How to research a problem
- How to answer technical questions
- How to communicate with angry customers

Skills and Activities
- Accessing customers on the computer
- Entering orders
- Reviewing customer history
- Processing returns
- Tracking packages

Ultimately, the biggest barrier to hiring has nothing to do with cash flow, though concerns about cash flow are often what we use as an excuse not to hire. Rather, when we find it difficult to determine what we need and when we need it, we can't make decisions. It is indecision, combined with the fear of making mistakes, which causes most business owners to delay hiring until the pain of not doing so is too great to ignore.

Now you have two important tools – a Skills SWOT and a Skills Matrix – to help you identify what you need. Using these planning tools will help you replace guesswork with confidence.

Prepare for the Hiring Process

If you want to increase your business value, hire the right people for the right roles. Easily said, not so easily done. There is a pervasive tendency toward *warm-bodyism* in the world of small business hiring. Warm-bodyism is the practice of hiring any warm body that seems reasonably stable and sufficiently competent to survive the interview. It is a result of waiting until the last minute and then hiring in a state of desperation. But you don't have to hire this way.

You can significantly increase your hiring success. Here are three important and easy-to-use tools. These tools will help you identify and document your needs, create meaningful job requirements, turn those requirements into effective Help-Wanted ads, and successfully place those ads in the right places to get you the most potential candidates.

1. Needs Assessment
2. PRO Job Description
3. The Meaningful Help-Wanted Ad

Nearly every business owner and manager can tell stories of their hiring mistakes. Most hiring mistakes happen when jobs are poorly defined, making it difficult to understand the specific qualities and skills required of the ideal candidate. But don't despair, and definitely don't avoid hiring! Instead, learn these crucial yet basic skills to help you identify and hire the best candidates.

Define Your Needs

Needs Assessment

Before you begin to think about the Help-Wanted ad, carefully assess your needs. Always start by evaluating whether or not a change in schedule, shuffling of duties, or additional training could eliminate the need to hire. If you truly need another person, ask and answer the following questions:

1. What business value must I gain from this person?
2. What responsibilities will this person be given in order to deliver that value?
3. What tasks will this person have to do to meet those responsibilities?
4. Which people/departments will this person interact with to meet those responsibilities?
5. Which personality attributes are best-suited to that work and those relationships?
6. Which skills must this person have to successfully complete the tasks?
7. Which background, education, and experience must this person have to successfully complete the tasks?
8. Does anyone currently working here have sufficient knowledge to provide the new person with training and development, or are we counting on this person to bring knowledge that we do not currently possess

in-house?

9. If this person is bringing knowledge we do not currently possess, how will I assess this person's skills and knowledge?

I recommend doing this exercise in writing. Writing forces you to think about and articulate your needs. Writing forces mental focus in a way that thinking alone does not, and for something as important as hiring, focus and clarity are a must. Besides, once you have completed your written list, you will find it very helpful for drafting help-wanted ads, preparing interview questions, and reviewing candidates with whom you have spoken. Don't short-change this process! The old computer adage *garbage in, garbage out* applies very well to the hiring thought-process.

When you have a very clear document that answers each of these nine questions, you will know that you are ready to move to the next step.

Write a PRO Job Description

Once you have compiled your Needs Assessment, you will have enough information to develop a reasonable job description. I'm not a proponent of traditional, static job descriptions. The typical job description is simply a laundry list of tasks with no context or clear purpose. Instead, I have developed a Purpose and Results-Oriented Job Description (PRO Job Description). Reflecting on the *purpose* of the job assures that the candidate understands and embraces the value he or she is expected to contribute. Describing *results* instead of just activities helps the employee to maintain focus on the expectations rather than just the tasks. Incorporating what you just learned about the four types of knowledge required (Company, Theoretical, Practical, Skills & Activities) ensures that each employee will have a comprehensive understanding of what is required and expected. A PRO Job Description looks like this:

Job Title: Head Buyer for Fashion Retailer

Job Purpose: Provides merchandise for customers by finding new sources, managing and maintaining relationships with existing sources, purchasing goods, providing information and training to sales staff, and liaising with key customers who have special merchandise needs.

Essential Job Elements

Plan for Inventory Needs
   Study needs, preferences, and buying patterns of customers. Determine which products are needed, at what price levels, and in what timeframe.

Results Expected: 4X overall turn, 43% overall margin, less than 5% backstock/out-of-stock.

Company Knowledge Required: Approved vendors and how to approve a new vendor, what customers expect in terms of product quality and prices, the company brand and which products fit/do not fit that brand, how we expect products to be delivered, what the other departments require to do their new product processing, display, and stocking tasks.

Theoretical Knowledge Required: Product Management Body of Knowledge, Supply Chain Management, Knowledge of the fashion industry and how the industry works.

Practical Knowledge Required: How to analyze sales and inventory results and market activity and use that analysis to identify desirable new products. How to find sources for those products.

Skills and Activities: Pulling computer reports and assembling data. Advanced spread sheeting. Data analysis. Internet, Trade Show, and Competitor observation and research.

Manages Open-to-Buy
Purchases within the dollar and unit guidelines as directed within the company strategy.

Results Expected: Stays within parameters of cash-flow budget, 4X overall turn, less than 5% backstock/out-of-stock

Company Knowledge Required: Cash Flow planning, inventory budgets, profit and loss statements, how to coordinate with accounting department to process and approve invoices and agree upon terms with vendors.

Theoretical Knowledge Required: Cash Flow Planning and Budgeting

Practical Knowledge Required: How to manage the forecasting and order placement/timing to meet company inventory needs while staying within a cash flow plan and budget.

Skills and Activities: Use the company computer system to create buying plans. Construct spreadsheets to create buying plans. Read and understand a Budget. Read and understand a Cash Flow Plan.

Develop New Products and Sources
Study the market, conduct research, network, travel to trade events, travel to specific markets, attend professional trade activities, and engage in conversations that lead to opportunities to buy desired inventory

Results Expected: 150 new products per year, of which 40 make it to the Top 20% sellers.

Company Knowledge Required: Which trade associations the company belongs to and the benefits they offer, past associations with trade organizations and why they are not currently being pursued, company philosophy regarding how it wants to deal with vendors and establish new vendor relationships.

Theoretical Knowledge Required: Market research, source development.

Practical Knowledge Required: How to work a trade show, how to negotiate new source agreements.

Skills and Activities: Book travel economically and effectively using company approved online resources. Use Evernote to capture trade event images and impressions in real time. Use Expensify to capture travel expenses and produce expense reports.

Approves Product Deliveries
Review inventory to ensure quality and quantities, review receipts, and authorize payments

Results Expected: 24-hour turn-around on receipts of inventory held back for quality concerns. Less than 1.0% return rate (from customers) due to quality problems. 0 days late in approving invoices for payment.

Company Knowledge Required: company quality standards, company accounting/payment procedures, company procedures in terms of who receives inventory and their procedures for getting inventory from the dock to the shelf.

Theoretical Knowledge Required: What counts for quality in this industry and company. UCC (Uniform Commercial Code) guidelines and implications.

Practical Knowledge Required: How to direct and monitor checking for quality standards. Maintain report cards or some form of measurement system to monitor vendor performance.

Skills and Activities: Pull reports on vendor performance, set up vendor reporting systems for other members of the organization to use. Use Adobe Digital Signature to send approved documents to Accounting for payments.

This job description may include several other responsibilities, including:

Resolves Discrepancies

Provides Product Information

Maintains Professional and Technical Knowledge

Identifies Current and Future Customer Requirements

Prepares Special Reports

Prepares Sales Staff

Each of those responsibilities would include the now-familiar elements of:

> Generic description of the responsibility
>
> Results Expected
>
> Company Knowledge Required
>
> Theoretical Knowledge Required
>
> Practical Knowledge Required
>
> Skills and Activities

After each of the responsibilities has been completely described, there is a Summary Section for results and each of the four types of knowledge:

Summary of Results Expected

- 4X Turn
- 43% overall profit margin
- Less than 5% backstock/out-of-stock
- Less than 1.0% return rate for "quality" issues
- Etc.

Summary of Company Knowledge Required

> This is a one paragraph summary of the company knowledge required in each of the responsibilities.

Summary of Theoretical Knowledge Required

> This is a one paragraph summary of the theoretical knowledge required in each of the responsibilities.

Summary of Practical Knowledge Required

> This is a one paragraph summary of the practical knowledge required in each of the responsibilities.

Specific Skills and Activities List (this is a bulleted list, rather than a summary paragraph) comprised of the skills and activities listed in each of the responsibilities:

- Read and use budget
- Read and use cash-flow statement
- Pull reports from company computer system
- Create spreadsheets in excel
- Use Evernote
- Use Expensify
- Use Adobe Digital Signature
- Etc.

Supervisory Responsibilities

- Inventory Control Administrator

The PRO Job Description requires more effort than any other type of job description, but the results are profound. Creating your PRO Job Description provides a roadmap that you can follow for every other step of the hiring process.

My best explanation for how valuable the PRO Job Description is compared to standard job descriptions is an analogy to baby furniture. Seriously. When my children were born, we bought them traditional cribs. After a while, we packed the crib away and we brought out the toddler bed. Eventually, we bought them regular beds. None of the sleeping apparatus had a life beyond its predetermined stage. In contrast, when my first grandchild was born, we bought her a wonderful bedroom set. When she outgrew the crib, the sides came down, the bottom dropped nearly to the floor, and it converted to a toddler bed. Later, the sides came completely off and became the headboard and footboard for a full-sized bed. This furniture grew with our grandchild, and twelve years later she is still sleeping in her original bed (frame).

The typical job description spends more of its time in storage than it does in use. But a PRO Job Description has a usefulness in every phase of a job, from its conception through its evolution.

Initially, you will use this format to describe what the job requires. This process will help you identify the skills, competencies, and characteristics of the person you will hire for that role. Next, you can use this format to help you create your help-wanted ad. After that, you will use it to help you design your interview questions, and as you will see in the section on orientation and training, you will use it to onboard[3] your new employee and help him take responsibility for his own success. This format will help you prepare your assessments of the person(s) in any role, and as a role evolves, you will update the PRO Job Description to reflect the changing nature of the job.

Once you have completed your Needs Assessment and your PRO Job Description, you are ready to start looking for

---

[3] Onboarding is a term used for the process of welcoming, training, and assimilating a new employee. Companies with Onboarding programs have higher rates of success in assimilating and keeping new employees.

employment candidates.

The Meaningful Help-Wanted Ad

Most Help-Wanted ads are slapped together at the last minute, often copied from some other company's help-wanted ad for a similar role. Please give your help-wanted advertising a little more respect than that.

If selecting a spouse required writing a Spouse Wanted Ad, you'd probably put a tremendous amount of time and thought into what you were looking for in your happily ever after. When you bring a new employee into your company, you are looking for someone you can trust to do the work, represent your company, behave well with your other employees, and appreciate your culture. This is a new relationship; perhaps not as significant as a spouse, but certainly more serious than choosing someone to go to the gym with.

Divide your help-wanted request into three sections:

- Personal attributes
- Skills and abilities
- Previous experience.

Personal Attributes

Before you create your ad, remember that it is easier to train someone to do a task than it is to train someone to be responsible, disciplined, or emotionally sound. You need healthy humans in your environment, so don't be afraid to ask for them. Up to this point, we've focused all our attention on what people need to know to do their jobs. But the Meaningful Help Wanted Ad starts with the behaviors and qualities you seek for your company.

Consider the type of personality that will do best in each role. If you seek an accountant, you don't require someone who is bubbly or extroverted. However, if you are hiring a sales person, you definitely need someone with good people skills and a desire to interact with other people as a major part of his job. If you are hiring an employee to do full-time training, you probably don't need a person as detail-oriented as the person you would hire for an inventory control position. If your environment is extremely collaborative, mention that you seek someone who likes working in teams.

Does it *go without saying* that you seek someone who is honest, hardworking, loyal, a good communicator, or accountable? I don't think it should. Say it. Say what you are looking for. Not only does it help employees know what you value in a person, it also tells them something important about your company.

Summarize the personal characteristics you seek in a paragraph. This will help potential candidates steer themselves toward - or away from - your job, which will save everyone involved a lot of time and potential angst.

Skills and Abilities

Be specific in your skills request. Most people will say yes to the question "Can you use Microsoft Excel?" So if super-spread-sheeting is what you need, make sure you request an Excel Super User. The list of people who will claim that status is significantly smaller than the list of people who claim to "know" MS Excel. Terms like *master, journeyman,* and *apprentice* can be helpful when seeking manufacturing or production applicants. A graphic artist with commercial art school training is likely to bring a very different perspective to the table than a self-taught graphic artist with a fine art background. If a skill that you require has a very broad range of interpretation, be as specific as you can be. If you ask for a diamond setter, you may end up with candidates that can only do prong settings in a production environment. If that's not sufficient, list the specific styles of diamond settings, or say that you need someone who can excel at six or more styles of diamond setting. Specificity regarding skills will help potential candidates self-select and reduce the risk of time-wasting.

Previous Experience

Some roles require previous education, others require relevant experience. In all cases, be clear about the type of experience you seek. If you ask for *a BA in Art or equivalent,* few people will interpret the phrase "or equivalent" the same way. It would be better to say that you seek "an art degree or six or more years functioning in a design or design apprentice role." When you create this requirement, question it. What types of experiences in work or education are likely to have honed a candidate to the point where they are ready to make a meaningful contribution in your business? If you can think of a person or two who has the types of skills you seek, ask them what their background involved and how it prepared them for the work they do today (who knows - maybe they're interested in coming to work for you!).

Why You Want to Work for Us

Another important element of any Meaningful Help Wanted Ad is what the ad shares about your company. Share some information about your values and philosophy. Let potential candidates know about your benefits package. Provide any information you can that entices potential candidates to consider you as an employer. Remember that you are not only competing against other employers for a candidate's attention – you may be competing with the candidate's current employer. It takes a lot of motivation for someone to consider shaking up his or her world and move to a new job, so make sure you provide that motivation in your Meaningful Help Wanted Ad.

Different Ads for Different Media

Before you attempt to write the 50-words-or-less job ad for your local newspaper, write a four-paragraph job ad with one paragraph for each of the sections discussed here: Personal Attributes, Skills and Abilities, Previous Experience, and Why You Want to Work for Us. When your word-count is limited, it's easy to include the wrong information. If you start with a fully developed description of the job, selecting the main points for a short ad will be much easier. Plus, many job posting environments will allow you to display your full description.

Put the long description on your website. Send it to your social media contacts and ask them to forward it to their networks. Post it on public bulletin boards. Send it to local adult and higher education outplacement offices. Take advantage of online and industry job sites, and search for any other outlet that allows longer-form ads. When you distill it for your newspaper, be sure to include the most important thought from each of your four paragraphs.

Be patient, and be prepared to play the numbers game. Hiring is time-consuming, and you must be prepared to keep looking until you find the right candidates for the interview process. Yes, that was candidates, plural. The chance that you will find the right person for the job in one interview is slim-to-none. If you have armed yourself with the tools and information we have discussed so far: a strategic awareness of your need, Skills SWOT, Skills Matrix, Needs Assessment, and a PRO Job Description, you are prepared. You are ready to interview, have meaningful insights, and select the best candidate for your company. All this preparation would be wasted on just considering one person!

Reviewing Resumes

I pity any job-seeker tasked with writing a resume. The seemingly simple exercise of listing one's previous jobs, responsibilities, and education has been morphed into an art form that can only be entrusted to professional copywriters. Much of this has been driven by HR professionals who feel beset by the number of resumes they must review. The world of job seekers has been told that they have two seconds or less for their resume to grab someone's attention.

We can do better than this.

It is the *job* of the hiring manager or HR department screener to find the right candidates. Just as it is the job of a head merchant to search in every nook and cranny to find the products that her competitors have overlooked – the products that will create huge wins for her company – it is the job of the hiring manager to find the most exciting, relevant, highest-potential candidates for her company.

Perhaps, if what you are seeking to hire is a professional copywriter, then you should care deeply about the construction, the *salesmanship*, of the resume. But if what you are hiring is an innovative product development person, a genius at keeping outdated machinery alive, an accountant who can read between the lines, or a manager with amazing motivational skills, then look for those things.

Read the resumes you receive. Read all of them. Look at the information they convey. Sure, pay attention to spelling and grammar and any other indications that the candidate possesses the skills you require. But spend more time considering the content of the resumes than whether or not they are formatted to your preference or take up two pages rather than one.

I equate this current rage for requiring the perfect resume with the Doctor's office wait. Patient scheduling is all about Doctors' convenience. Make the patient wait, because the Doctor must not. And finally, the healthcare system is beginning to realize that this is not a good formula for patient satisfaction. Likewise, it's time for hiring managers everywhere to do our jobs. It's not the job of the candidate to bring us the perfect canned resume. It's the job of the candidate to tell us where they worked, what they did there, what type of education and training they have pursued, and why they should be considered for our opportunity. And it's our job the diamonds, even when they are in the rough.

Should We Use a Pre-employment Assessment?

What is a Pre-employment Assessment?

Pre-employment assessments, sometimes referred to as talent assessments or employment screening tests, are psychological assessments that can be used to enhance the hiring process. Most of these assessments have been designed using hiring and retention case studies, performance data, and other employment information that cumulatively lead to predictive analytics about who may or may not be successful in a given role.

Using a pre-employment assessment tool can be very useful. Unfortunately, many companies that use these tools in their hiring practice use them inappropriately or ineffectively. A pre-employment assessment is most effective when it is used to help you develop questions to ask in an interview – not as a stand-alone hiring decision-maker. A well-designed, psychologically and legally vetted assessment tool can provide tremendous insight into the cognitive ability, motivations, working behaviors, potential, personality dimensions, and cultural fit of a candidate.

Over 2,500 pre-employment assessments are on the market – a market that is estimated at over one billion dollars per year. This demonstrates how important pre-employment assessments have become to business in general, and also illustrates how many options one has in selecting a provider. Rather than telling you which pre-employment assessment provider to use, I'll offer the following suggestions:

- Unless you have a psychology or extensive Human Resources background yourself, hire an expert to help you select the proper tool for your business, and use that expert to teach you how to interpret and use the tool you select.[4]
- Verify that your expert is truly an expert in Human Resources and psychological assessment tools, and not just a generic business advisor. Interpreting a pre-employment assessment requires extensive training and experience. Be sure that what you are paying for is depth of experience in the use of these tools, and not just a computerized model that you are left to interpret for yourself.
- Ensure that any tool you select has been peer-reviewed by the psychological testing community and that it is considered to be free of bias (racial, ethnic, gender, etc.).

One of the most important roles your expert will perform is to help you select the right test for your purposes. It is not uncommon for a company to use an improperly matched pre-

---

[4] StrategyWerx, a brand owned by Andrea Hill, provides pre-employment assessment services for small business owners using IPAT assessment vehicles.

employment assessment, and then be dissatisfied with the results. For example, one of the most well-known personality assessments today is the Myers-Briggs Type Indicator (MBTI). Many companies have used it as a pre-employment assessment tool. While the MBTI is a terrific assessment to use for employee development, it is not a good predictor of job success. Of greater concern, it is not a *qualified* vehicle to use for that purpose. The Myers-Briggs publisher warns that "it is unethical and in many cases illegal to require job applicants to take the Indicator if the results will be used to screen out applicants."

A pre-employment assessment comes with potential legal and discrimination risks. Following the suggestions above will help protect you from those risks and, more importantly, ensure you are using the best possible tool in the best possible way.

The Role of the Pre-employment Assessment

The decision to hire or not to hire should never be made on the basis of a pre-employment assessment alone, and the pre-employment assessment should be neither the first nor the last step in your hiring process. It belongs in the middle.

It may help to reflect on this fact: The interviewee has the most power in a job interview. It may seem as though the interviewer has the power, because the interviewer will decide whether or not to hire the candidate. But the interviewee is entirely in control of whether or not to tell the truth and how much of the truth to tell.

I once asked members of an audience to raise their hands if they considered themselves a poor judge of character. Though over 400 people were present, only two hands went up. Then I asked a show of hands for how many people had ever willingly entered into what turned out to be a bad relationship. Not surprisingly, nearly every hand went up. We all think we are good at reading body language, sensing a person's mood, or determining if another person is warm, cold, honest, or high-maintenance. But psychological studies indicate that our first impressions of others are colored by our personal filters – our own personalities, experiences, relationships, expectations, and quirks – so we may not actually see the other person until we have spent several dozen hours with them.

Most hiring decisions are made after less than one hour of interaction.

That's scary, given what you just read.

The use of a well-designed pre-employment assessment will give you deeper insight into the person you are considering. This insight will lead you to explore more aspects of the candidate's work behavior, their past work experiences, motivations, and interpersonal skills than your uninformed perspective could have led you to question.

Many excellent hiring processes take place without pre-employment assessments, and many sub-par hiring processes take place with the aid of pre-employment assessments. I am a big fan of using pre-employment assessments, but only if the criteria and process described here are used diligently.

Pre-employment Assessment Example

Most providers of pre-employment assessments take the raw data from the applicant's test, process it, and produce canned reports that suggest likely behaviors and patterns. Sometimes these canned reports are too canned. The best assessments provide additional raw data that your service provider can use to supplement and enhance the canned reports.

Be cautious about companies promoting inexpensive online skill surveys that you implement yourself. Look for a service provider that offers some nuance in the reporting, and expect to pay $100 - $225[5] per assessment. Does that seem expensive to you? Consider that the U.S. Department of Labor estimates that it costs $40,000[6] to hire an employee that makes $20,000 per year, or that the cost of a hiring mistake is estimated to be between $25,000 and $50,000. A few hundred dollars up front is a small price to pay for increasing your hiring and retention success rate in the long term.

The type of report your provider should produce will cover

---

[5] The estimated costs in 2014

[6] This figure includes everything from advertising and interviewing through training costs, salary and benefits.

topics such as cognitive ability, interpersonal communication style, how the candidate handles stress, the candidate's learning potential and learning style, aptitudes, team-orientation, attitudes toward authority, autonomy, initiative, self-control, and motivational style.

The best providers will also offer guidance regarding what types of questions to ask and specific areas to probe for further consideration of your employment candidate.

The following is an example of a partial report from pre-employment assessment produced from the data provided by a 16PF[7] assessment from IPAT[8].

Candidate:	John Q. Candidate
Summary of Positive and Negative Considerations	
Positive	Mr. Candidate appears to be very intelligent, self-reliant, and self-motivated. He appears to have the ability to maintain personal discipline while juggling many responsibilities in a challenging role.
Negative	Mr. Candidate's strong need for autonomy and his trust issues may interfere with his ability to collaborate with others, take direction, or keep his superiors informed about what is going on. Mr.

---

[7] The Sixteen Personality Factor Questionnaire (or 16PF) is a multiple-choice personality questionnaire which was developed over several decades of research by Raymond B. Cattell, Maurice Tatsuoka, and Herbert Eber.

[8] IPAT is a provider of assessments used for pre-employment, career counseling, and therapeutic applications.

Candidate appears to be motivated to accrue personal power.

General Characteristics

Impact on Others	Mr. Candidate tends to be discreet and cautious about revealing personal information. This can make him seem secretive, thus placing a distance between himself and others. Even those who interact with him regularly may feel there are sides of him that they do not know. People also may notice that he rarely seeks advice or support from others. Thus, superiors may only learn about problems he's faced or decisions he's made after the fact. **Explore this Area** Even the best and brightest need input and collaboration from others. Make sure Mr. Candidate is interested in and willing to participate in collaboration. Otherwise he will stagnate as a professional and alienate people as a peer. Ask questions like: • Please describe one of your best experiences of collaboration. • Who do you go to when you are unsure how to solve a problem? • How quickly do you alert your employer or supervisor when something is going wrong?
Interpersonal Stress	It appears that Mr. Candidate has a basic underlying mistrust of people. If this is accurate, he may be seen as quick to take offense or as "having a chip on his shoulder." At times, he may misconstrue others' motives or alienate them by jumping to negative conclusions about them too quickly. Overall, he may be seen as fairly calm, mature, and easy to get along with, except in frustrating or stressful situations. **Explore this Area:** The person in this role must be able to remain in a positive mental space about the people he or she serves. If the person in this role is quick to jump to

conclusions about users intentions or abilities, then the support will be colored by that perception or he may become frustrated with their questions.

- He should be asked to describe how he has handled situations in which users asked particularly troublesome questions, needed a lot of extra training, or couldn't understand why they were doing things the wrong way.
- He should also be asked how the people he has supported in the past would describe him as a support person.

Power Dynamics	Mr. Candidate is in the average range on assertiveness and is generally not controlling about trying to get others to do what he wants. However, because Mr. Candidate is also self-sufficient and usually prefers to rely on his own judgment in making decisions, others have less control over him.
Social Orientation	Mr. Candidate derives an average amount of gratification from interacting with people as an end in itself. His scores also indicate that he has a wary and vigilant attitude toward people. This could be justified or even adaptive if it is limited to specific individuals or if he is living in a hostile environment. However, if neither is the case, his approach to people may be hampered by a lack of basic trust. He may be somewhat ambivalent, liking and wanting to be close to people, but questioning their sincerity and intentions. **Explore this Area:** Ask Mr. Candidate, "How easy or difficult is it for you to trust your teammates to do something as well as you would do it?" Ask Mr. Candidate, "Please tell me about a time that a peer or teammate made a mistake that affected you or your work. How did you feel about it? How did you handle it?
Working	Mr. Candidate tends to be self-reliant and generally

Alone or With Others	prefers to function independently. He may be best suited to an employment situation that does not require close teamwork but does involve some contact with people.

The actual report would have contained many more characteristics, and would have been 6-8 pages in length.

Should I Discuss the Assessment Results with the Candidate?

No guideline exists regarding whether you should or should not share assessment results with a candidate. Though it is increasingly common for hiring managers to put the assessment results in front of the candidate and discuss them openly, it's not the norm.

If your pre-employment service provider also provides a service for reviewing assessment results with candidates, or if you feel competent to and comfortable with discussing the results, it can be a very gracious thing to offer after-the-fact. Or, if you want to put the assessment results on the table as part of your long interview and explore them openly with the candidate, this is also an option.

From a process standpoint, I recommend using the results to develop the questions for the long interview, but not making the assessment results the centerpiece of that interview. One way to do this is to preface questions with something like:

> "*Your assessment results indicated that*
> _____, *so I want to explore this by asking*
> *you if* _____."

It takes a particularly experienced person to present personality assessment results in a non-threatening, morale-building manner that provides clear direction even on the less positive aspects. If you don't have this expertise, you probably shouldn't experiment.

The Interview Process

Have you ever heard the saying *first you solve the process, then you solve the people*? It's one of my favorites, because it reminds us that much of what we view as a failure at a personal level is actually failure at a process level. If a process is broken, or missing, unfortunate mistakes can happen.

Interviewing is not an event, it is a process. When done correctly it includes multiple steps. These steps are designed to build on one another, helping us to layer on impressions and experiences that lead to a better hiring decision. If you follow these process steps, you will extract maximum value from your interviews. The steps include:

- Phone Interview
- Short Interview (30 – 45 minutes)
- Pre-employment Assessment
- Long Interview (1+ hours)

Start With the Telephone Interview

The first step in your hiring process should generally be a very brief (15 minutes or less) telephone interview. Chatting on the phone with candidates will help you make quick decisions about whether or not to invite them for a formal interview. Prepare two or three questions to ask of each candidate in this phase. These questions can include:

- What is it about this job that appeals to you?

- Which requirement in the job ad do you think best applies to you?

- What are you looking for in your next job?

Do not try to engage in questions about past experience or skills during the short telephone interview. If you do, it will no longer be a short interview, and those types of questions are best answered face-to-face. The telephone interview is merely a way to set the stage for a short in-person interview and to weed out candidates who are clearly not a match. If you decide to invite the candidate to an in-person interview, explain to them that you will be spending 30-45 minutes with them, and that after your short interviews you will decide which candidates to invite back for a longer interview. Do this whether you have two, or 20, candidates to consider.

The Short Interview

During your short interview (we will discuss interviewing techniques and questions in the next chapter) you will decide whether or not to invite the candidate for a long interview. The short interview is intended to accomplish two things: Establish the facts about a candidate's skills and experience, and create a baseline impression of the candidate.

Observe him carefully. Does he appear to be comfortable sharing information about himself? Does he seem to be candid? Has he arrived for the interview appropriately dressed and groomed? Does he present himself with seriousness and professionalism?

> *Does it really matter how a candidate dresses for an interview? What if the position involves working on a dock or operating heavy machinery? It still matters. The candidate need not appear in a suit, but his appearance should indicate that he takes the interview seriously and prepared himself for it. I always like to see a candidate appear in clothing that is more formal than what he would expect to wear while working. Even if your culture is extremely casual, introduce him to that once he is hired. Let him try a bit harder at this stage.*

Why does the short interview focus primarily on previous experience and skills? First, because if the candidate doesn't have the type of experience you seek, or doesn't appear to be a good prospect for developing them, it doesn't make sense to dig deeper. Second, because putting space between the short interview and the long interview provides time for the reflection and planning needed to effectively explore issues related to motivation, behavior, and potential.

Have you ever interviewed someone for a position and then later, when you were reviewing your impressions, you had several doubts or questions that you wish you had clarified at the time? If you only conduct one interview, then these doubts and questions are troubling. But when you follow this process of interviewing, the short interview provides insights that you will explore in more depth during the long interview.

Pre-employment Assessment

It is between the short interview and the long interview that you should conduct the pre-employment assessment. When used properly, the pre-employment assessment will provide you with information about the candidate that you should explore in more depth during the long interview.

For example, a pre-employment assessment may indicate that a candidate appears to be much more comfortable working alone than as a member of a team. This may lead you to ask questions that require her to provide examples of times that she worked within a team, and to discuss what went well and what could have gone better.

Or, a pre-employment assessment may suggest that a candidate doesn't handle criticism well. You may want to explore this in more detail by asking her to describe a time that she received criticism and how she responded to it. You will also want to ask her questions regarding her relationships with former managers, and look for clues as to whether or not she was willing to accept direction from them.

After you have conducted your short interviews and you have identified a candidate (or hopefully several) that you think may be a good fit for the job, you will ask them to participate in a pre-employment assessment. After the assessment has been completed, you will use the assessment results to design specific interview questions.

What if You Don't Use a Pre-Employment Assessment?

If you choose not to use a pre-employment assessment, you will still use the time between the short interview and the long interview to review your impressions and develop questions that you will ask in the long interview.

When I was younger I was very proud of my ability to make decisions quickly, and the ability to make fast decisions certainly plays a role in being a successful entrepreneur. But when it comes to considering the merits and possible shortcomings of other human beings, I have become a fan of *sleeping on it*.

After a terrific short interview, you will be flush with excitement about the candidate. It's only later – that evening, or the next day – that concerns and questions may come floating in. Write these things down, and prepare to explore them during the long interview.

Similarly, you may interview a candidate who possesses all the experience and skills you require, but the interview leaves you flat. Taking time to sleep on it will help you evaluate your own reactions. Is your response to the candidate more about you than about her? Or are the concerns real? Do you actually require chemistry with this hire for them to be successful?

Whether or not you use a pre-employment assessment, the

time between the short interview and the long interview will give you the opportunity to ponder the candidate, make a list of her pluses and minuses, and review your own filters for faulty judgment.

The Long Interview

The long interview is your last chance to ask all the questions you need to ask. How long is long? It depends on the position for which you are hiring and the importance of that role to your company's success.

Plan to spend a minimum of one hour in your long interview. And this is a bare minimum. For professional candidates, you may wish to spend half a day or more. Include spending some time together outside the interview, such as lunch, and you will get a much better experience of the candidate than an interview alone can provide.

Some positions require an extended skills assessment. Many high skilled production environments (such as a jeweler or tool and die maker) will pay a candidate for a day of work in order to fully assess his skills. This day should also include an interview of an hour or longer.

I'm a fan of long interviews that create a zone of familiarity and comfort, interviews that inspire the candidate to disclose more about himself than he would otherwise be inclined to do.

Your goal throughout the interview process is to develop the most thorough, accurate assessment of what a candidate is capable of contributing, how a candidate is likely to behave, and whether or not the candidate will fit within your environment. This process is designed to help you cultivate those answers and lead you to the best possible hiring decisions.

How to Interview

The saying be *careful what you ask for, because that's what you'll get* is particularly true when it comes to hiring. The most important tool in your hiring toolbox is your interview skills. Unfortunately, the job interview as most people know it is a very poor excuse for a conversation, let alone a significant hiring decision.

5 Critical Requirements

Throughout the interview process you must carefully explore these five things, which I refer to as the 5 Critical Requirements:

1. **Skills**: If the candidate possesses the skills you are seeking, how he learned those skills, and how long he has been using those skills.

2. **Work Ethic**: If the candidate has a good work ethic. Is he responsible, accountable, disciplined, self-motivated, and concerned with doing things the correct way?

3. **Relationships**: If the candidate gets along well with others, shares information as appropriate, takes responsibility for his share of the work, and is interested in pitching in to help others when needed.

4. **Character**: If the candidate behaves in a positive way. Does he avoid gossip and negativity, and will he do

his part to create an enjoyable workplace? Is he trustworthy, honest, and forthright?

5. **Potential**: Is the candidate capable of growing as the role/responsibilities grow? Is he bright, an inquisitive learner, and engaged?

This extended interview process gives you the chance to engage with the candidate more than just once, which has more potential to reveal important aspects of his personality than a one-interview approach offers.

The Telephone Interview

This interview is as difficult for some people as cold-calling, and in fact, it is a form of cold-calling. It can be intimidating to pick up the phone and call someone with whom you have never conversed before. People tend to put off what they find intimidating.

Don't put this off! If cold-calling isn't your thing, it may help you to prepare a short script before you make these calls. Give yourself an outline of what you want to accomplish.

It might look like this:

Hi! My name is _____

I'm calling about the _____ you applied for.

I just have a few short questions to ask you, to see if it makes sense for us to set up an in-person interview.

- What is it about this job that appeals to you?
- Which requirement in the job ad do you think best applies to you?
- What are you looking for in your next job?

If you feel like giggling right now, you're probably not one of the people who finds it difficult to pick up the phone and call someone unknown. But for those who do find this difficult, providing yourself with a script can mean the difference between making those calls today or two weeks from now.

> Get out your notebook!
>
> *From the moment you begin talking with candidates, you must keep copious notes. Don't try to keep all your ideas, observations, and questions in your head. Write notes while you're interviewing, and write your thoughts in-between interviews. These notes will be invaluable to you when it's time to make a decision.*

Remember, you want to keep these phone interviews short. Everything else you ask the candidate, you want to ask while he is sitting in front of you. So follow your script, make a decision, and schedule a time for him to come in for his short interview.

How to Conduct the Short Interview

The short interview is primarily a fact-based interview. During this interview you will concentrate on the candidate's skills and his training and work history. Your goal is to ascertain that the candidate will be capable of doing what you need him to do as quickly as possible after hire.

> *Kindly but insistently push interviewees to be specific. This is something you will do repeatedly throughout the interview process.*

Make sure you have studied the applicant's resume carefully prior to this interview. When you are managing an interview, you need to be focused on what the candidate is saying and not on the piece of paper. Ask questions like:

- Please tell me about the education and training you have received that qualify you for this position.
- How many years of experience do you have in this role or skill, and in how many different jobs have you been responsible for this role or skill?

Ask the following questions about each of the jobs they had previously:

- Tell me about your job at _____. Please describe for me a typical day/week in that position?
- What were your responsibilities in that position?
- Who did you report to in that position?
- How many people worked in your department?

- Did other people have the same role as you, or were you the only one doing that role?
- Why did you leave that position?

After developing an understanding of the candidate's training, experience, and detailed job history, probe any gaps in employment and the reasons for those gaps.

Other elements you should explore in the short interview include:

- Ask the candidate to describe, in detail, how he does particular tasks related to the job. Even if you are not an expert at doing that work yourself, you can certainly assess whether or not the candidate is speaking with enough specificity to indicate genuine skill in that area. If the candidate is vague or generic, dig deeper. Kindly but insistently push interviewees to be specific.
- Ask the candidate to describe a success or contribution he is particularly proud of in a previous job.

Make sure you ask if the candidate has ever been fired from a job, and *why*. Don't assume just because someone has been fired that they are not hirable. Many good candidates have been let go from a job, and they grew tremendously because of it. Ask the candidate to describe what he learned from that experience, and listen carefully to his answer.

Remember that there are some questions you are never allowed to ask in an employment interview. Inquiries about race, religion, citizenship status, marital status, children, pregnancy, gender, and disabilities are unacceptable. A guideline to keep in the back of your mind is that a question you wouldn't ask of *everyone* is probably not a question you should ask of *anyone*.

Skills Testing

If specific skills are required, use a skills test. A skills test is the only true way to assess capabilities, and the more technical or complex the skills required, the more important a skills test will be.

If there are 2,500 pre-employment assessments on the market, there must be 10,000 skills tests. In some cases you must create your own. If you are hiring a master bench jeweler, CAD designer, sketcher, tool & die maker, machine operator, or other skilled artisan, you probably want to create a skills assessment related to the type of work your company produces.

If you are hiring someone to provide computer support, there are hundreds of online assessments that will ask specific questions and score the candidate's answers. These can cost anywhere from $25 - $200, depending on the skill.

You can purchase online spelling, math, grammar, and keyboard skills tests for as little as $2 each. Several companies now provide Microsoft Office testing to help you make sure the candidate really has the skills she says she has, and these tests are often as low as $20 each.

Particularly motivated candidates, in professions as diverse as gemology, graphic design, and computer sciences, will bring certifications along to attest to their skills.

At the end of the short interview you should have a strong understanding of the candidate's previous experience and whether or not his skills are sufficient to be successful in the role for which you are hiring.

How to Conduct the Long Interview

The long interview is primarily a behavioral interview. In this interview you will concentrate on categories two through five of the 5 Critical Requirements; work ethic, relationships, character, potential.

Establish a conversational tone during the long interview. It is important for the candidate to be as comfortable as possible, because people reveal more about themselves when they feel secure. If you have used a pre-employment assessment, you will go into your long interview with questions designed to probe specific aspects of the candidate's personality, working style, and behavior.

You will also prepare for your long interview by considering your observations from the first interview (remember, if you did not do a pre-employment assessment, this will be your primary type of preparation for the long interview). Was the candidate fidgety? Reluctant to answer certain questions? Were any of his answers lacking specificity or depth? Prepare questions to elicit the clarifications you need.

Begin by asking questions designed to provide insight into work ethic, interpersonal skills, character, and potential. Here is a short list of questions that will help you develop insight in these areas:

- *How often have you been late for work in the past month? How often are you late in the course of a year?* Listen closely to his answer. It will not only tell you the bare facts of his attendance, it will also reveal to you the value he places on punctuality.

- *Have you ever taken personal responsibility for a problem created by your team or department? Why or why not? If you did, please describe the situation.* This is a question intended to reveal aspects of character related to accountability. Employees who feel responsibility for the results of their work group – and not just themselves – are better team players and tend to demonstrate a higher sense of ownership.

- *Please rate this answer on a scale of 1 to 7: I finish my work on time. (1 = never, 7 = always).* One of the things I always look for when I ask this question is whether or not the candidate pauses to actually think about it. I'll take a sincere "almost always" over an automatic "always" any time.

- *What pushes your buttons (makes you irritable or angry) at work?* Everyone has buttons, and mature people are conscious of them. The candidate's answer should reveal to you a sense of self-awareness and a willingness to be candid about his shortcomings.

- *Please describe the last time you thought of an opportunity for improvement in the work place. What was your idea, and what did you do with it?* It's not enough to have ideas – you are looking for employees who have ideas and look for ways to implement them. Of course, many workplaces do not encourage their employees to come up with ideas (a sad thing), but highly motivated candidates will still have an example or two of trying.

- *How would your peers rate you on this statement: "He chips in and helps even if it's not in his area?" (1 = never, 7 = always).* The 'it's not my job' attitude is death to morale and productivity. The way the candidate answers this question will help you look for that attitude.

- *Describe something new - personal or professional - that you have learned to do or understand in the past year. Why did you decide to learn, and how did you go about learning it?* People who are curious and engaged in life look for new things to learn. They also make the best employees. The answer to this question will shed light on the candidate's interests, and will also teach you something about how he acquires new skills.

- *What do you think about the statement: "You can get things done right, or you can get them done fast?"* You are looking for people who don't believe a sacrifice on either end is necessary. Candidates who don't believe you must sacrifice speed for quality, or vice-versa, will tend to look for solutions that include both.

- How would your peers at your job/former job describe you?

- What personal attribute do you think your former boss appreciated most about you?

During the next phase of the long interview, explore the questions that came from the pre-employment assessment process and the questions that occurred to you when you reflected on the short interview. This is where those notes you've been keeping come in handy! You should have had lots of ideas for questions to ask when you reviewed your notes from the short interview.

Finally, here is my list of 11 All-Time Favorite Interview Questions, developed over more than 25 years of looking for fantastic employees. Save these questions for the last part of your long interview, and you'll find that by the end of them you have a much better sense of who the candidate is and whether or not you want to work with him.

My 11 Favourite Long Interview Questions

1. *Describe the most creative thing you have done in the past*

year. If you want engaged employees, you want people who consider their own lives to be interesting and worth engaging in. What you're looking for in this answer is (a) the ability to choose something quickly and (b) a degree of enthusiasm about the creative pursuit.

2. *What would your peers say about you?* Ask each candidate to imagine for a moment that in your search for a reference you approached his peers instead of his previous boss or HR department (or classmates, if you are interviewing a very young person). You are looking for a sense of how the candidate functions in a team and if he is conscious of his impact on others in his peer group. Most people have a sense of how to defer to authority, so true interpersonal skills and deficiencies tend show up at the peer level.

3. *Please describe your decision-making approach.* Ask the candidate to describe how he goes about making difficult decisions (you may want to use an example, such as buying a car or buying a house). Then, ask him to describe his decision-making approach in comparison to his peers. While you listen to the answer, listen for the following attributes. Is the candidate (check all that apply)?

[ ] Decisive and quick
[ ] Sometimes too quick
[ ] Very thorough
[ ] Sometimes too slow

[ ] Intuitive
[ ] Inclined to go purely with facts
[ ] Inclined to involve many people
[ ] Inclined to involve few people

4. *When presented with a new idea or skill that you must master, how do you go about learning it?* No single learning style (visual, auditory, kinesthetic) is superior to another, and most people can't tell you which one they favor. What you are looking for is that the individual understands how he goes about mastering something, because this indicates whether or not he will be a self-motivated learner.

5. *Please describe a situation in which you were pressured to compromise your integrity, and how you handled it.* Any person old enough to have a work permit has experienced at least one situation like this. You are looking for how well-formed his ethical thinking is. Contrary to popular thought, much of our ethical development occurs in our late teens and young adulthood – not in our childhood. So be prepared for young adults with only a fuzzy grasp on ethics, and look for indications that the young adult has a character foundation and is interested and trainable.

6. *Other than your parents and grandparents, who have your greatest influences been?* The answer to this question reveals what type of mentorship this person gravitates to – if any. People who won't or can't learn from others will be difficult to train and develop over time.

7. *Five Strengths/Five Weaknesses.* You know the question "Please tell me one weakness you have." Get rid of it. Most of the time you'll get an ingratiating response regarding how they are a workaholic or a perfectionist. Instead, take a hint from business thinker and writer Marcus Buckingham and ask "can you tell me five of your strengths and five of your weaknesses?" Sure, you may get *perfectionist* and *workaholic* as two of their weaknesses, but they'll have to work harder for the other three. This answer provides tremendous insight regarding how self-aware this person is and whether or not he is capable of and willing to be honest and a bit vulnerable.

8. *Please describe your most significant accomplishment in your career to date.* The answer to this question reveals character, personality, ability to learn, team skills, ability to accomplish results, pace, attitude, capability and potential. Look for results achieved and the process used to achieve those results, and try to develop an understanding of the environment in which the accomplishment took place. If you are hiring a young person, let him answer this in terms of a school, camp, sports, or other group accomplishment.

9. Prepare a job-specific, realistic problem that the candidate will be dealing with in the job for which the candidate is interviewing. Describe the problem in some detail. Then ask the candidate *"How would you*

handle this problem if you were to get the job?" Listen to his answer carefully, and if he hasn't already addressed the following things, prompt him for:

[ ] How would he go about organizing it
[ ] What resources would he need
[ ] What would he do in the first few weeks
[ ] What problems would he expect to encounter
[ ] How long would it take
[ ] What would he do first

10. *Describe five things about the training, communication, or atmosphere of this company that need to be present in order for you to feel satisfied and successful working for us.* You can't find the right employee if you don't know what that means – and the same is true for your job candidates. You are looking for indications that the candidate is conscious of his role in achieving a good fit. If he is going to be entirely passive in this regard, he certainly won't be engaged.

11. *How would you finish the statement "People are . . .?"* Never ask this question until very late in the interview process. You want your candidate to be relaxed and feeling like it's nearly over. The reason this question is powerful is reflected in the saying *we don't see things as they are, we see them as we are.* Even if the interviewee has been conning you with socially appropriate answers (which hopefully you have been able perceive), his answer to this question will reflect his general opinions about others and some truth about

himself. As with everything else, though, be sure to interpret the answer in context. I once heard an interviewee respond immediately with the answer, "People are dishonest!" Did that mean he was dishonest? Not at all. He was a retired law enforcement officer, and his answer reflected all his years of experience.

With these 11 questions you can assess the candidate's peer relationships, decision-making, learning, problem-solving skills, ethics and character, self-awareness, motivation, and general outlook. But please don't assume these 11 questions represent a complete interview. They are just 11 questions that you should be certain to ask, in addition to the questions you will ask regarding qualifications, history, and specific job requirements.

The interview process I designed for professional level candidates lasts a full day. When candidates express surprise at the length of time the interviewer wants to spend with them, I advise the interviewer to remind them that, if hired, they would likely spend years of their lives working together. Given the importance of everyone's time, it is well worth the expenditure of one day to ensure a good fit.

One final word about the interview process. You are supposed to be doing most of the listening, not most of the talking. It may surprise you to learn (it certainly surprised me) how many employers talk their way through an interview, selling the company, the culture, the products and services they offer, and generally doing everything but getting the candidate to open up. Reserve a few minutes to share a brief overview of the company and its culture and its products and services, and another few minutes to share the expectations and requirements of the specific job for which the candidate is interviewing. At the end of the interview, ask the candidate if he has any questions about the company. Other than asking questions and clarifying them as needed, this is all the time you should spend talking during an employment interview.

Recommendations and References

Two words: *Do this*. Do check the references of your employment candidates. Do ask if they have any letters of recommendation that they can provide. This is a simple, effective part of your hiring toolbox that is almost completely neglected today.

No doubt it is harder than ever to get good job references. The pressures of living in a litigious society have stifled the sharing of important information. There is nothing unethical, unfair, or illegal about sharing valid reference information about a former employee, but fear of legal action is a powerful thing. This doesn't mean you should stop trying to check references though. It means you should become a tenacious reference-getter.

Though there is a perceived risk that someone who is given a weak or negative reference will sue the reference giver, the incidence of such actions is actually quite low. In contrast, the risk that a candidate for employment will provide inaccurate information that inflates previous pay, overestimates their contribution, and exaggerates their importance is very high. This is why you must work hard to get the references you need, even if some of the reference givers seem reluctant.

If the former employer is a large company, contact the HR department prior to your reference calls and do your employment verification (confirm dates of employment and previous pay). HR departments will rarely offer anything other than a confirm-or-deny response (they will only answer *yes/no* questions), but that's all you need from them. Unless your candidate was an employee in the HR department, you'll need to speak to his former manager or direct supervisor to receive the meaningful insight you require regarding his character, personality, skills, or work ethic.

Once you get the basic employment verification, there are a handful of questions that you should ask every time you talk to a reference. These can be modified to suit the specifics of the job for which you are hiring, or you can add your own.

1. *What were the responsibilities this candidate had while he was employed by you?* Always start with this question. It's an easy question to answer, it's nonjudgmental, and it allows the reference-giver to gather her thoughts about the candidate – with whom she may not have worked in some time.

2. *Is the candidate more independent or more of a team player?* This is another good question to ask early in the interview, because unless the reference has strong opinions about whether one or the other is preferable, it is a nonjudgmental question. The answer, however, is important to you. Think carefully about what you need, because if you don't know whether the role for which you are hiring requires independence, teamwork, or both, the answer will be meaningless.

3. *How did the candidate get along with peers? How did he get*

along with subordinates? How did he get along with management? If you just ask "how did the candidate get along with people," you won't uncover any potentially interesting patterns with regard to authority, competitiveness, or power. So look for relationship behavior clues by asking the question in three parts.

4. *How would you describe the candidate's performance related to* _____? Fill in the blank with a characteristic that is important to the role for which the candidate is being considered. You may ask this question as many times as you have specific characteristics to explore.

5. *How would you describe this candidate's dependability?* Look for responses to both the candidate's attendance and his ability to get things done. If the reference only answers to one of those issues, prompt for the other.

6. *Did the candidate meet his business objectives, and can you describe a specific accomplishment?* Ask this as a two-part question. It is too easy for the reference to say, "Oh, yes, yes, he met his objectives." If the reference has to think about specifics, she will provide you with a less superficial answer.

7. *How did the candidate respond to your efforts to suggest or assist with professional or personal development? And what types of professional or personal development were recommended during his employment?* You are looking for whether or not the candidate is likely to be open to

input from you and if he values opportunities for improvement. There are few things more frustrating than hiring someone who isn't open to learning or changing.

8. *How would you describe this candidate's strengths?* If the reference only offers you one strong quality, prompt for a second, or even a third if you think the call is going well enough to dig a little deeper.

9. *How would you describe your management style, and how did the candidate respond to your style?* This question is most helpful when you have asked it of multiple references for the same candidate. Comparing the answers can provide a fairly comprehensive picture of how a candidate responds to being managed.

10. *Why did the candidate leave your employment?* Many times the answer given by a reference will differ slightly from the answer given by the candidate. When you compare the reasons, you can see if they are two perspectives of the same issue, or if the candidate was possibly unwilling to tell his former employer the whole truth. Don't assume dishonesty if the answers are different. Look for how the two parties could genuinely believe what they believe. But clearly, if an employer says the candidate was fired or was asked to find alternative employment and the candidate hasn't told you this, it's a red flag.

11. Now take a moment to describe the position for which

you are hiring. Describe the basic responsibilities and the primary expected outcomes of the job. Think about this carefully before you call – too often people don't know how to describe a job succinctly, and the description drags on. Once you have described the position, ask: *Do you think the candidate is a good fit for the job I have described?* Make sure you probe the answer to understand *why* or *why not* if the reference doesn't offer the reasoning behind her answer.

12. *Would you hire this candidate again?* Every reference expects this question, and if they are giving a negative reference, they are probably dreading it. But your conversation so far will have made it much easier for the reference to answer honestly. Make sure you probe for why or why not if their reasons have not already been made clear.

13. *Based on the information I shared with you, should I hire this candidate?* This is always an interesting question to ask. Some references won't answer just because they don't like to speculate in that way. But there's no harm in asking it, and the answers can be quite insightful.

Set aside enough time to make reference calls, and make sure you are relaxed and in comfortable control of the discussion. There is nothing more awkward – speaking from the perspective of someone who has given numerous references – than being called and asked for a reference, only to find out the caller is unprepared to manage the conversation.

Don't let one very positive reference tempt you into not calling the others. Reference checks are most valuable when you can compare and contrast the responses, and it is highly likely that the references have had different experiences, even if the differences are subtle.

When "Yes" and "No" Are Your Only Options

Sometimes you will encounter a reference who tells you "I'll answer yes or no questions only." If someone says this to you, don't be deterred! Be prepared, and ask the following questions:

1. Did this candidate have good knowledge in the area of _____ (the skills you are hiring him for)?

2. Was this candidate responsible for _____ (the things he told you he was responsible for in that job)?

3. Did this candidate consistently show up for work on time?

4. Did this candidate do his work as you expected it to be done?

5. Did this candidate get along well with his peers?

6. Did this candidate have any problems with authority?

7. Was this candidate an effective and thoughtful manager/supervisor of others (if applicable)?

8. Was this candidate good about receiving critical feedback?

9. Did this candidate leave the position because _____ (whatever reason the candidate told you)?

10. Would you hire this candidate again?

Finish by asking if there is anything else the reference thinks you should know.

During this yes-and-no conversation, listen as closely to what is not being said as to what is said. Some references will be Spartan with their responses simply because they have been advised by their legal counsel or human resources department to do so, but nobody refrains from offering a glowing reference.

There are few things more important than the quality of the people you hire. Most hiring managers understand the importance of careful resume review, good interviews, and background checks. But the process cannot be considered complete without reference checks, because the reference check is generally the only avenue you have to investigate and confirm the candidate's claims.

What's In a Background Check?

Most employee background checks include a Credit Report, a Criminal Records review, Drug Tests, and Employment

Verification (which should be done as part of the reference checking process).

The Fair Credit Reporting Act (FCRA) sets the credit standards for screening for employment, and in order to run a Credit Report you must receive written authorization from the employment candidate to do so. Laws vary from state to state regarding checking criminal history, and some information cannot be disclosed without the candidate's consent. If you plan to run criminal or other background checks beyond the basic Credit Report, I advise that you seek the advice of a local human resources expert first.

Background, credit, and drug testing can provide important insight regarding a person's personal habits, self-control, and discipline. But remember that there are often important stories behind a candidate's bad luck. If every other aspect of the employee's job interview, pre-employment testing, and reference checks is positive, and you see some negative information in the background check, ask the candidate about it. The answers he gives and the discussion you have will give you even greater insight into whether or not to hire him.

Making the Offer

Boy oh boy oh boy is this one of the hardest aspects of hiring, particularly for small business owners. Pay is such a personal, psychological, personal (redundancy intended) thing, and in a small business, it's just as personal for the owner. I have noticed two pay-personality types in my small business owner world.

Type A: She is worried about having too little to offer, about offending someone with less than they expect, and about being able to keep paying enough more, year after year, to keep the new employee satisfied. She is deeply concerned with keeping her employees happy and making sure they feel valued, and she wants to be confident her employees' pay is sufficient to create feelings of happiness about the job.

Type B: This owner feels a bit resentful about paying an employee. She recognizes that she does not pay herself enough, and almost feels put-upon when an employee asks for a specific wage. The process of deciding what to pay someone feels like pressure or an imposition. She knows intellectually that her employees will not and should not work for free, but emotionally that's precisely what she wants.

Whether you are Type A or Type B or (more likely) somewhere in-between, the solution to the emotional weight of what to pay is the same. You create a salary benchmark for each PRO Job Description. You can hire an expert to create this for you, or you can do it yourself. The challenge is to acquire the appropriate data to create your benchmark.

What is a salary benchmark? A salary benchmark is a statistically valid range of pay for a specific job in a specific region. It takes into account the type of business you are and the size of your business. It is typically divided into quartiles, with the lowest pay for that job in the first quartile, and the highest pay for that job in the fourth quartile.

Many trade associations create salary benchmarks for their industries, and salary information can also be found through survey tools like the Economic Research Institute Compensation Assessor (ERICA) or the professional (not consumer) tools from Payscale.com. If your industry does not have pay range data available, it is probably less expensive to hire someone to create a few select salary benchmarks than to subscribe to the expensive tools (like ERICA or Payscale.com, which can cost several thousand dollars each year) necessary to acquire the data to create benchmarks yourself.

A salary benchmark provides an objective, informed baseline for what you should offer for a particular job. People with the least experience, at the lowest skill level for a functional area are compensated in the first quartile, and people with the most extensive and sophisticated experience are compensated in the fourth quartile. Compensation always has a strong element of subjectivity to it, but working with a salary benchmark will give you a framework within which to apply that subjectivity.

Salary benchmarks change over time - and they don't always

go up. For instance, if a profession has a glut of workers available compared to the number of jobs, the salary range may actually go down. Salary benchmarks can change due to overall economic conditions, supply and demand of labor, new technology, and competition from other regions or countries. Most companies that use salary benchmarks review them every two or three years.

Once you know the reasonable range of pay for a specific job, you must determine what the actual pay for a candidate will be. This process begins with you. Consider everything you have learned about the candidate, from his job history and skills to his demeanor during the interview and his answers to the more personal and challenging questions you have asked. Decide which quartile of the salary benchmark for this job best applies to this person. You may end up a bit higher or a bit lower, but start by picking a quartile that reflects what you think his true value will be to the organization based on your experience with him so far.

Next comes a question. Ask the candidate, "Do you have a salary amount in mind for this job?"

Assuming that the job you have to offer is similar to or a step up from the job the candidate already has (or most recently had), most candidates will give a number that is both reasonable for the job and truly indicative of their needs and expectations. Just as the primary grocery shopper for a family usually knows the cost of milk and bread, job seekers know the market for their particular skill. One rule here: If a person asks for pay below the salary benchmark, at least pay him the minimum of the benchmark. If he sincerely qualifies for the job as it is described and benchmarked, he qualifies for at least the base level of pay. This will help keep your pay equitable and your employees satisfied.

I can hear several of you asking right now, "But what if he asks for pay that is above the benchmark?" While there are exceptions to any rule, be quite sure if you make this exception that it is truly worth it.

My term for paying someone above the salary benchmark is *golden handcuffs*. Chances are, the employee being paid more than his job is worth in the market cannot get an inflated rate of pay for his skills somewhere else, so an employee with golden handcuffs may stay in a job past the time when he is happy, and therefore, productive.

If you have a candidate that is so amazing he can take your company to the next level while baking cookies for his coworkers and being a never-ending delight to work with, then perhaps you want to offer him what he's asking. Chances are, your feelings aren't that strong. It just feels uncomfortable to offer someone pay that is lower than what they have asked for.

This is where your salary benchmark comes in and helps you strip the subjectivity back out of the process. Assuming your salary benchmark was created with good data, you have reliable information about what a specific role is worth in your market.

example of what a job benchmark may look like

Benchmark   **Job Title or Name**

Brief description of primary job responsibilities goes here. Jobs are benchmarked primarily on tasks rather than titles, which can be arbityrary. May be shown as hourly or annual.

Quartile 1	Quartile 2	Quartile 3	Quartile 4
$21,435 - $26,392	$26,393 - $32,437	$32,438 - $36,729	$36,730 - $40,121

If the only feeling you have about offering a lower number than what is being asked for is fear of rejection (and not the I-can't-live-without-this-guy-in-my-business   feeling),   then proceed as follows:

1. Explain to the candidate that your salary benchmark for this role does not go that high.
2. Take a fully conscious moment to reflect on the quartile you originally selected for this candidate.
3. Make your offer.

You have used every tool at your disposal - from the definition of need and description of job to a thorough interview. You know what the job pays in your market and you have a sense of what this candidate is worth to you. Make your offer knowing that you have done everything in your power to make a reasonable offer, a good offer. The candidate may want to discuss it, and you may or may not feel there's room for discussion. Let your gut guide you.

In addition to pay, make sure you discuss any benefits you have to offer, including the opportunities for and rules about vacation and personal time off. Benefits have a financial value, and you should know the financial value of your benefits so you can speak about them in terms of both what they are and what they are worth. Some candidates will accept a lower rate of pay in exchange for additional days of vacation in the first year, or in exchange for the ability to work longer hours on some days and half days on others.

It's hard to anticipate all the negotiating points that can come up during an employment discussion. But once you have reached an agreement, be sure to document it. This does not need to be an employment contract (in fact, I advise against that). Rather, it's a simple memo with a bulleted list of the things you agreed upon as your terms of employment. And if all goes well, you have a new employee and it's time to put him to work!

Raw Ingredients Really Matter

My in-box is a petri dish of engaged workforce issues. I see inquiries ranging from business owners wanting advice on how to cultivate engaged workforces to employees wanting to know how they can influence their bosses to include them, and everything in between. At some level, even the most autocratic boss recognizes that employees who care about doing a good job deliver more profit than employees who do not. But how do we cultivate this? The answers involve every aspect of your business, but let's focus on a narrow area of significant importance.

Imagine for a moment that you have taken a two-week culinary class at one of the most prestigious cooking schools in the country. Now you're home, and hosting a dinner party for a few of your best friends. Your guests know where you've been, and they are expecting an exceptional meal. Do you buy the cheapest ingredients you can find to make your dinner? Probably not.

There is nothing more important than the raw ingredients we start with in business, yet there is an astounding lack of understanding regarding how to hire them.

The ability to hire the best people is one of the most important, under-rated, misunderstood skills in the books of business knowledge. Improving hiring skills is one of the most important things a small business owner can do.

The Basics of Basic Training

I have taught a number of children to drive, so I'm no newcomer to beginning driver training. Even after all that practice, it can be stressful at best, and sometimes harrowing. But the process – when well done – is an excellent model of training. Students are required to gain a certain number of hours behind the wheel, accompanied and instructed by a responsible adult. In many states the students are required to keep a training log of hours, whether those hours were done at night or during daylight, and how much time they drove during each session. Once they pass a driving test they are given a provisional drivers' license, which gives them privileges to drive, but with restrictions.

All of this makes sense, right? Not only do we want to protect our children, but we also want to protect the other drivers on the road. When training is this close to home, we take it very seriously.

So why are we so flippant with business training? We bring a new employee in, we throw him into a job with somewhere south of an hour of orientation, and we expect him to be successful. This isn't good for the driver or the other drivers on the road. Failure to provide new employees with excellent training can lead to job loss and economic hardship that might not have occurred had they been properly assimilated. Other employees suffer because their new colleague is not as efficient or effective as they need him to be. Nobody's interests are served.

Assuming a highly trained or long-experienced professional will not require training is also unfair. So much of learning to do a job well is learning the culture and practices of the company, and those things vary dramatically from organization to organization. Just learning the acronyms specific to a business or industry requires a pocket handbook that, to my knowledge, no company ever provides.

There's very little business knowledge I would take from most State Departments of Transportation, but I think the driver training model is a good one to emulate. Establish what it means to be a good driver, provide a structured training model to create and foster good driving skills, make sure there is time to practice, and have people already successful in the role monitor the learning and development. Apparently, this model is desperately needed in business, because United States voluntary turnover rates are over 23%, and involuntary turnover adds another 10-12%. That means that companies are losing 33 – 45% of their employees annually. The cost of finding new employees and assimilating them to the point of full contribution is generally figured at two years of their full starting salary.

But you don't have to suffer these statistics, because you have created a PRO Job Description for your new hire, and you are now going to use that document to create your training plan, including goals and objectives for the new employee introductory period (sometimes referred to as probationary period) which is typically the first three months.

Before your new employee's first day on the job, review his

PRO Job Description carefully. For each element of the document, determine what type of training will be required for the new employee to be successful. The training can be classroom training, reading specific materials, job shadowing, or on-the-job instruction. What they are supposed to learn, how, and from whom, should be very clear.

Next, set Goals and Objectives. What must this new employee accomplish in order to be successful? How much time in training and assimilation will be required before that success is possible? How do you plan to measure the employee's success? Write down each of these goals and objectives, and prepare to share them on his first day of work.

Your new employee needs these clear goals and objectives on his very first day because you start paying him on his very first day. The sooner you help him understand what success looks like, the sooner he can begin pursuing that success. Review with him his PRO Job Description, and discuss his training plan. Specifically, tell him what you expect him to master in the first, second, and third month, and explain to him the training that is available to him to achieve that mastery. Tell your new hire that he will participate in a progress review at the 30, 60, and 90-day marks, and that the review will specifically assess how well he has achieved the goals and objectives discussed on this first day. Spend time that first day talking about role expectations and how he is to get the help he needs to be successful. Some people may find this process intimidating. In fact, when it's done well, it's incredibly liberating. No guesswork is necessary to figure out how they will be successful.

Is this hard work? Yes, it is. But think about it: If you can't articulate what is expected from your new employee, his resources for training, and how you are going to measure his success, then how can you expect him to make meaningful and fast progress in his new job?

Feedback Feedback Feedback

As I write this book we are training a new puppy. He has so many things he needs to learn, from getting outside to go to the bathroom to leaving my shoes and kitchen rugs alone. Puppy training success is entirely dependent on feedback. We recognize him with praise and treats every time we catch him doing something right, and provide gentle but immediate feedback when he does something wrong. Long ago, when I started my family, I noticed that raising children required many of the same elements - praise when you catch them doing something right and gentle but immediate feedback when they are doing something wrong. As it turns out, we don't change much as we age. The recognition, rewards, and tone of voice change, but the fundamental need for feedback never goes away.

Feedback is the most important training you can provide your new employees. Of course, to provide affirmation and recognition when they are doing the right things and gentle but immediate redirection when they are doing the wrong things, you must be *paying attention*. I can hear your inward groans now. Yes, you hired this person so you would have more time to do your own thing. But the payoff is not immediate. You must plan to spend an appropriate amount of time reinforcing the behaviors and skills you require and redirecting the behaviors you don't if you want that employee to ultimately step up and provide his full value.

This is not an invitation to micro-manage. If you micro-manage your new employee, you will never learn whether or not he knows to do the right things in the right ways. Rather, it is a reminder to observe, be available, encourage questions, and observe some more. If you have properly prepared your new employee with his PRO Job Description, goals and objectives, and a training plan, he should be able to demonstrate that he is capable of and willing to progress rapidly in his new role.

Be Specific with Positive Recognition

The most common form of positive recognition most employees hear is "good job today!" or "good job on that project!" This type of feedback is nice, but hardly motivating. To provide people with meaningful recognition, your praise must be specific and timely. Which feedback would you prefer?

Feedback A: "You did a great job on that project!"

Feedback B: "Good job bringing in that project on budget. I particularly appreciate how hard you worked to interpret the customer's needs and give them exactly what they wanted. That showed a lot of creativity and sensitivity on your part."

The feedback given in Feedback B is packed with information. It shows your employee that you were truly paying attention - which is a form of praise all by itself. Feedback B also highlighted a specific set of behaviors, practically guaranteeing that the employee will be conscious of doing those things again on the next project.

Be Calm and Direct with Corrective Feedback

I enjoy observing parents on playgrounds, because one learns so much about the human condition. Have you ever noticed that there are two types of parental response to a child falling down and hurting herself? Overly Sensitive Parent reacts by acting shocked and sad that the child is hurt and adds drama to the situation. Pragmatic Parent provides a bit of practical comfort, assures the child that she is OK, and encourages the child to resume her play as quickly as possible.

It's the Pragmatic Parent you want to channel when giving corrective feedback, but many people channel the Overly Sensitive Parent instead.

The Overly Sensitive mode of corrective feedback leads to a lot of internal dialog and stress regarding how the feedback should be given, when it should be given, and worries about how the employee will react. The Pragmatic Parent mode of corrective feedback is simple and direct. You approach the employee and say, "Hey, I observed such-and-such, and that's the incorrect way of doing that. Let's review your training so it can be done correctly the next time." This is done in a calm, non-judgmental, matter-of-fact tone that carries no emotional repercussions. Like the child of the Pragmatic Parent, the employee picks up on your okay-ness and moves forward without drama.

Giving effective and consistent feedback is one of the most important things a company can do to improve new employee integration. Most people want to do a good job, in their interpersonal relationships and in their work. Our employees deserve to receive the feedback that will help them accomplish that.

Onboarding

You wouldn't invite an outsider to a house-party full of close friends and then leave her to fend for herself. You'd take her around and introduce her to everyone, share some information about what each person did for a living or was interested in, and help initiate a conversation.

It's no different with a new employee. Take the time to make introductions, tell the new employee about each of his new workmates and what each person is responsible for. Make sure he knows where the bathroom is, where coffee is available, kitchen etiquette, what everyone does for lunch and breaks, and who to ask for which type of help.

Does this seem like an unnecessary instruction to you? Then you'd be surprised to find out how many new employees suffer through their first week just trying to figure out the ropes, let alone their new jobs!

We've covered two of the most important elements for starting an employee off on the right foot – training and feedback – but there is so much more you can and should do to ensure your new employee is assimilated as positively and as quickly as possible. We call this overall process of welcoming, preparing, and assimilating new employees *onboarding*.

Formal or Informal Onboarding?

Some companies use informal onboarding, a casual guideline they use to introduce all new employees to the company. As long as it's not as casual as *sink or swim*, a casual approach can be perfectly sufficient.

Other companies us a formal approach to onboarding. Formal approaches include checklists and policies, and the onboarding process for each new employee is reviewed for compliance.

The choice of a formal or informal process is entirely up to you. You should decide this based on your company culture and your overall discipline for implementing and maintaining new processes. If you're generally good at making sure something gets done once it's agreed upon, then an informal process may be all you need. If your organization tends to get excited about something one day, then forget all about it the next, a formal process may be in order.

Regardless which approach you take, your onboarding program should include the following elements.

Organizational Norms

Every company has norms, some formal and some informal. The formal norms are typically documented in the Employee Handbook, which should be given to each employee on her first day of work. New employees should be instructed to read the Handbook and indicate (usually by returning a signature page) that they have done so within the first few days of work.

Other formal norms include how to petition for vacation days, policies regarding unplanned days off, attendance, where and when to take breaks, dress codes, security, and other dos and don'ts.

Informal norms can be harder to articulate. They tend to arise in context, and are often not thought of until someone violates one. This is why I recommend using a Buddy System as a vital component of your Onboarding program.

Buddy System

One of the most effective ways to assimilate a new employee is to assign a Buddy (or Mentor or Guide – whatever terminology works for you). Avoid making the manager or supervisor the Buddy. The manager is responsible for training, feedback, and performance. In contrast, the Buddy is responsible for guiding the new employee through the social and cultural aspects of his new job. A new employee is more likely to ask a peer questions about how to assimilate than a manager, and you want those questions to be asked.

Each person who takes on a Buddy role will need to be trained in the Onboarding elements of your organization. This comes with an exciting additional benefit: Any person who performs as a Buddy ends up having a stronger understanding of the cultural and social fabric of your company. It is this type of ownership that contributes to stronger employee engagement.

Cultural Knowledge

Every business, no matter how large or how small, has a culture. It may not yet be the culture you want, it may have evolved organically, but it is a culture, and your new employee needs to understand it.

Business culture is made up of many attributes. For instance, are you more customer focused, more product/innovation focused, or more cost/efficiency focused? Is your environment highly collaborative or do you foster more inter-personal competition? Are you fairly hierarchical in your structure or more casual and flat in your management approach? What is the communication style and norms of the company, and how much is communication encouraged?

It's your job to describe the culture you have. If it's not the culture you want, then you must also articulate where you want the culture to go. This description should exist in a formal document. It can include a mission statement, your business purpose, and elements of your brand. It can be a statement of principles by which you want your company to operate. Once you have done the work of formalizing your statement of culture, it's ready to be shared.

In some organizations, the owner or primary business leader

introduces the culture to every new employee. In other organizations this is done by the Buddy. Either way can be effective. If you have done your work of describing the culture you want to have and how you want that culture to continue to evolve, that description can be passed from one person to another successfully.

When you take time to explain and discuss your culture with each new employee on the first day, that employee receives a significant head start in understanding not only how the company does things, but also why the company does things the way it does.

Social Integration

The Buddy becomes key to a new employee's social integration. Sure, some new employees are comfortable just jumping in and discovering how things work, but most people appreciate a little guidance. The Buddy covers the basics of showing the new employee where the bathrooms and the coffee station are, and when to take breaks. The best way to accomplish this is to introduce the Buddy to the new employee early on the first day[9] – as soon as you are finished reviewing the training plan and setting goals and objectives. The Buddy gives the new employee a tour, showing the new

---

[9] Some companies introduce the Buddy to the new employee in advance of the first day, so the new employee arrives already knowing someone and with an expectation of how the first day will be spent.

employee where everything is, and introducing the new employee to the people with whom he will interact (or everyone, if your organization is small enough to do so).

The Buddy's role extends through the first 90 days of employment. During the first week the Buddy will accompany the new employee on breaks and lunches and grease the wheels of new business friendships. As the new employee becomes more comfortable, the Buddy remains available to answer questions and provide support. Any employee may be confronted with a unique or challenging situation that requires a little advice. Having a Buddy available to help with these situations can help prevent an employee from derailing.

Make the First Day Special

Do your best to make the first day special for your new employees. Have a sign at the front door welcoming the new employee by name. Make sure he knows what time to arrive and who will be waiting for him. Make sure the appointed person *is* waiting, and knows what to do next.

Depending on the amount of hiring you do and your budget, consider ordering in lunch on an employee's first day. This makes the day special for everyone, and eating together is an important form of social glue.

What's going on behind-the-scenes can have a significant effect on how special the new employee's first day is. Every person who will work or interact with the new employee should know what day he is starting and what his job will be. Unfortunately, I've witnessed new employees being grilled on the first day with questions like, "when were you hired?" "What were you hired for?" and statements like "Nobody told me you were starting!" Even if such comments aren't intended to be mean-spirited, they are still terribly uncomfortable.

If someone internally was competing for the job, that person should have been informed privately not only that she didn't get the job in question, but who did, and your reasons for choosing the person you chose. You may not be able to eliminate hard feelings, but you can honor those feelings by addressing them in a forthright manner.

Be as creative as you can be in making a new employee's first day special. After all, it is a special day! You have done so much work to find the right candidate, and this person is bringing your company exciting new potential. Why wouldn't you want to celebrate that?

If You Have to Cut the Cord

One of the most difficult things we deal with in hiring is discovering that we have made a hiring mistake. This is bound to happen once in a great while, even if you have done everything else right. If you use the principles taught in this book, you can reduce your risk significantly, but you can't eliminate it. So how do you know if it's time to cut the cord, and when do you do so?

How Do You Know?

The reasons for new hire failure are probably evenly divided between employers and employees. On the one hand, employers can do a poor job of training and assimilating new employees, and on the other hand, a certain number of people will successfully over-sell themselves into positions for which they are not qualified. Most of us will second-guess ourselves about letting someone go, because we understand that our decision will land someone on the street without a paycheck. We will want to give that person a little more time, help them try a little harder, and hope that the situation will turn itself around.

The framework you have learned in this book - creating the PRO Job Description, developing a training plan, establishing goals and objectives, and observing closely - will make it much easier for you to not only recognize fatal shortcomings in your new employee but also to feel sure about your observations. When you are confident that you have provided everything you can to facilitate success, when you have carefully observed your new employee's progress relative to the plan you laid out with him, and offered meaningful feedback along the way, then letting someone go still doesn't feel good, but it also doesn't feel wrong or unfair.

Successful employment is a two-way street. The employer has a responsibility to do everything she can to set the stage for success, and the employee has a responsibility to take advantage of the tools and support that have been provided and make success his own.

The *when* is easy. If a new employee is not the right choice, make that decision as soon as it is clear to you. Don't put it off. A clean, quick break is much less painful than an extended period of dissatisfaction and anxiety for you, your new employee, and the rest of your employees.

What if you are the Problem?

Being a good leader means developing excellent listening and communication skills, keeping your ego in check, cultivating creativity, serving as a role model, being a motivator through positive behavior and encouragement, and being passionate about your business and your people.

Sometimes, the one thing standing between a business owner and an engaged, successful workforce is . . . the business owner. We human beings are very good at getting in our own way, and one of the ways entrepreneurs undermine themselves the most is by failing to become effective leaders and managers.

One thing you can do to evaluate yourself as a leader and manager is to take one of those pre-employment assessments yourself, participate in a personal development evaluation, or both. I have taken an MBTI (Meyers Briggs Type Indicator) and 16PF (IPAT Personality Assessment) every 3-4 years for the past 30 years. I have found these tools invaluable to me as I set personal and professional goals and track my progress toward them.

Use the results of these assessments to help you select leadership and personal development resources specific to your needs.

You can outsource many things in your business, but you cannot outsource effective leadership. This you must learn, and you must learn it sooner rather than later. Can you do it? Of course you can. But it takes work and dedication.

Postscript: Asking for Help

Help is a funny thing. We often – in fact, almost always at some level – need it. But we don't always get it. Is this because the universe is unkind?

No. It's because we only get help when we actively seek it, we only actively seek help when we genuinely want it, and *wanting* help is not the same as understanding we *need* help. I have known people who were aware for years that they needed help, but all the same did not want it.

The reasons for not wanting help when one needs it are probably as myriad as the genetic combinations that define us physically. Maybe we judge ourselves and think we shouldn't need help, or we think needing help is a sign of weakness. Maybe we struggle to accept that someone else knows something we don't know. Perhaps we worry what others will think, or we don't like the uncomfortable feeling of being helped. Maybe we don't believe that others will do things as well as we would. And the list goes on.

So why is this important? It's important because throughout our careers we all need help. We need assistance, people to whom we can delegate, people from whom we can ask advice, and people willing to tell us the truth. The people who achieve the most have something in common . . . they accept the necessity and value of help, and the reality that they cannot do everything themselves. They value help.

This doesn't just apply to one-man operations. I have met

many entrepreneurs with 20, 30, 40 or more employees who still insist on having a hand in every single aspect of their business. They are only satisfied when the people helping them are doing things exactly as they would, which is impossible. Those businesses are as hobbled as if the entrepreneur hadn't hired anyone.

The decision to hire, particularly when running a very small business, is a decision to ask for help. In some cases, business owners who need help and don't ask for it use the justification that they *can't afford it*. In reality, when someone genuinely wants help they always find a way to ask for it and acquire it. But the *wanting* – the accepting that we will be better with help than we are without help – must come first.

So ask yourself: In what areas of your life and business do you need help, and what is holding you back from seeking it? Once you have your list, do the inner work to figure out what's holding you back. Then go on . . . ask for help. You deserve it.

Free Forms and Tools

If you would like forms and tools to help you with your hiring process, you can download them at the StrategyWerx website.

Go to www.strategywerx.com. Click the "Resource Center" menu, and you'll find them there.

Seminars & Newsletters

Andrea Hill offers small business seminars and newsletters to help small business owners take their business to the next level. Stay informed about new books, resources, and events. Sign up for her mailing list at www.strategywerx.com

Index

8776015R00065

Made in the USA
San Bernardino, CA
24 February 2014